C000081402

THE DAWN
OF STEAM

A DEFINITIVE COLLECTION

BY ROBIN JONES

First published in Great Britain in 2009

British Library Cataloguing-in-Publication Data
A CIP record for this title is available from the British Library

ISBN 978 1 906887 28 5

PiXZ Books
Halsgrove House, Ryelands Industrial Estate,
Bagley Road, Wellington, Somerset TA21 9PZ
Tel: 01823 653777
Fax: 01823 216796
email: sales@halsgrove.com

An imprint of Halstar Ltd, part of the Halsgrove group of companies
Information on all Halsgrove titles is available at: www.halsgrove.com

Printed and bound by Grafiche Flaminia, Italy

Introduction

During the Industrial Revolution, mineral railways or 'waggonways' were commonplace, but only as 'secondary' systems transporting freight to and from the nearest navigable river, canal or sea port.

All that was to change with the invention of the steam locomotive, and it was Cornish mining engineer Richard Trevithick who sparked off the transport revolution which led to the modern age.

Britain led the world in steam engine technology, but while a few of the early landmark locomotives survived as museum pieces, many, sadly, did not.

However, several modern-day projects to build replicas of these lost locomotives have proved hugely successful.

This volume presents a complete guide to Britain's early locomotive fleet in the 21st century, featuring both original survivors and the modern replicas.

Austro-Hungarian army officer Nicholas Joseph Cugnot demonstrated the world's first steam tractor in 1769, but it was a clumsy affair that came to grief by turning over in a Paris street.

William Murdoch experimented with steam traction in Cornwall, and he infamously ran a 19in-long three-wheeled steam carriage one night along the lane leading to Redruth church. The machine ran loose at 8mph, terrifying the rector who believed that the devil was about to attack!

Trevithick increased the level of steam pressure in stationary engines so that he could make smaller versions – and realised if they could power a machine or pump, they should be capable of being adapted to drive themselves.

This was the great turning point – the greatest since the invention of the wheel itself.

Dedicated To Vicky and Ross

PHOTOGRAPHIC CREDITS
Grateful thanks to the following who contributed photographs: Paul Appleton, Ffestiniog Railway, Clive Hanley, Beamish Museum/Paul Jarman, David Langfield, National Museums Liverpool, Anthony Coulls/Locomotion, Museum of Science & Industry, Manchester, Andrew Naylor, Brian Sharpe, Great Western Society, Phil Trotter,.

Special thanks to Paul Jarman and Anthony Coulls for their help.

Special thanks to Paul Jarman and Anthony Coulls.

Over the past four decades Beamish: The North of England Open Air Museum in County Durham has emerged as a world leader in the study and recreation of early railways, and in 2008 laid a replica early horse-worked waggonway, complete with wooden rails.

Left:
A statue of Cornish giant of steam Richard Trevithick carrying a model of his 1804 locomotive inside the National Railway Museum at York.

Right:
Trevithick and engineer Andrew Vivian built a steam road carriage which, on Christmas Eve 1801, ascended Camborne Hill under its own power. Onlookers jumped aboard for a ride – making it the world's first motor car! The Trevithick Society's replica is pictured at the National Railway Museum's Railfest 200 event in 2004 at York.

Right: Trevithick overcame the problem of muddy potholed roads by using rails instead. In 1802, he built a railway locomotive for private use at Coalbrookdale ironworks in Shropshire. This working replica built by apprentices at GKN Sankey in Telford in 1989 is based at the Ironbridge Gorge Museum.

Below: In 1987, a non-working replica of the Coalbrookdale locomotive was built in Birmingham by Task Undertakings Ltd, supported by the Manpower Services Commission and the Prince's Trust. It is displayed at Telford Central station.

Trevithick then built a locomotive which helped ironworks owner Samuel Homfray win a 500-guinea bet that a steam engine could haul ten tons of iron over the horse-drawn tramroad linking Penydarren ironworks near Merthyr Tydfil to the Glamorganshire Canal. On February 21 1804, the bet was won after the world's first public demonstration of a steam locomotive. A replica built in Wales in 1981 from Trevithick's original documents and plans is now on display in the National Waterfront Museum in Swansea. It is pictured in action at the Railfest 200 celebrations at the National Railway Museum in 2004.

Left:
The original locomotive did not survive, but here is a section of the rail and stone block sleeper from the Penydarren Tramroad in the National Railway Museum at York.

Right:
The reverse of the £2 coin issued by the Royal Mint in 2004 to mark the bicentenary of Trevithick's first public demonstration of a steam railway locomotive.

Left:
Trevithick's last locomotive, *Catch-Me-Who-Can*, briefly ran on a circle of track in 1808 near the site of the future Euston station. Built at Hazeldine Foundry in Bridgnorth, Shropshire, by engineer John Urpeth Rastrick, with its carriage, it became the world's first steam passenger train. A marvellous working replica built in Bridgnorth by the Trevithick 200 group is pictured in September 2008.

Long hailed as the world's first drawing of a steam train, experts now believe that this painting of *Catch-Me-Who-Can* is a late 19th-century fake based on earlier sketches.

Left:
As he made little money from locomotives, Trevithick stopped building them, and the horse and cart still reigned supreme. New railways designed purely for horse traction opened, like the Stratford & Moreton Tramway in 1826: one of its wagons is displayed near Clopton Bridge in Stratford-upon-Avon.

Chronic shortages of horses due to the military needs of the Napoleonic Wars led to mine owners looking again at Trevithick's ideas. During 1813-14, engineer William Hedley, enginewright Jonathan Forster and blacksmith Timothy Hackworth built *Puffing Billy* for Wylam Colliery near Newcastle-upon-Tyne. The world's oldest surviving steam locomotive, and used until 1862, it is now in the Science Museum in London.

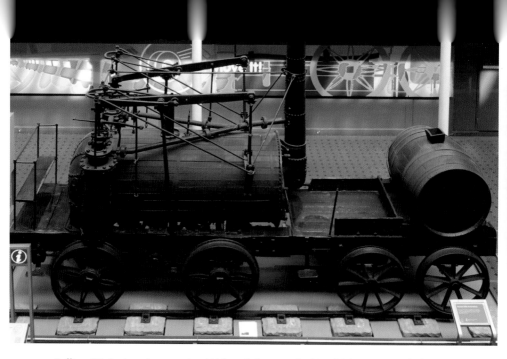

Puffing Billy's sister locomotive, *Wylam Dilly*, is in the Royal Museum in Edinburgh.

Not only did *Puffing Billy* encourage the development of more locomotives for the mines of the north east, which became the 'cradle of the railways', but it also entered the English language in phrases like 'puffing like Billy-o'. Beamish Museum unveiled its splendid working replica of *Puffing Billy* in 2006.

Left:
Using only a contemporary painting and basic sketches to produce a design as close to the original as possible, Beamish experts recreated the *Steam Elephant* of 1815 in 2006, to run on the museum's standard gauge Pockerley Waggonway. The original was designed by John Buddle and William Chapman for Tyneside's Wallsend Colliery.

Right:
George Stephenson built his first locomotive in 1815. Seven years later, with Nicholas Wood he constructed an 0-4-0 for Hetton Colliery in County Durham which remained in service until 1913. It is now displayed at Locomotion: The National Railway Museum at Shildon.

Dartmoor's fascinating Haytor Granite Tramway was among the last lines in Britain built for purely horse traction, but ironically has survived most other Devon steam era branch lines.

Built in 1820, its 'rails' are made from granite blocks, and it even has points and crossovers, just like a 'conventional' railway!

The 4ft 3in gauge tramway transported stone from the quarries at Haytor down to barges on the Stover Canal near Newton Abbot for transhipment onwards by sea, and was used until 1858. The stone was used to build London Bridge, part of the British Museum and London's old General Post Office.

A scheme to electrify the route in 1905 came to nothing.

Thanks to the durability of the granite rails, the tramway can be easily followed across the moor today. Two blocks are also preserved in the National Railway Museum at York.

September 27 1825 saw the Stockton & Darlington become the world's first to run public steam passenger trains. Its first locomotive was 0-4-0 *Locomotion No 1*, built in George and Robert Stephenson's works under Timothy Hackworth. It is now in Head of Steam – Darlington Railway Museum.

Left:
Beamish Museum built a working replica of *Locomotion No 1* in 1975.

Right:
Standing in the National Railway Museum at York is *Agenoria*, built in 1829 by Foster, Rastrick & Company of Stourbridge (the same Rastrick who built *Catch-Me-Who-Can*) and which worked at Shutt End Colliery near Birmingham for more than 35 years.

Foster, Rastrick built a near-identical machine, the *Stourbridge Lion*, for the Delaware & Hudson Railroad. The first locomotive to run on rails in the USA, Clyde Osmer DeLand produced a painting of it in 1916. The boiler and other parts are displayed at the Baltimore & Ohio Railroad Museum in Baltimore, while the Delaware & Hudson built a working replica in 1932.

The Rainhill Trials of 1829 was a contest to select suitable motive power for the Liverpool & Manchester Railway. However, it had far wider implications, for it decided which form of traction would be adopted by Britain's expanding rail network: at the time, cable haulage and horse traction were still considered serious alternatives! The judges were *Rastrick*, John Kennedy and Nicholas Wood.

The trials were 'restaged' at the Llangollen Railway in 2002 for the BBC TV programme *Timewatch – Rocket and its Rivals*, using modern-day replicas.

Pictured is a basic representation of *Cycloped*, a strange horse-powered locomotive entrant built by Thomas Shaw Brandreth of Liverpool.

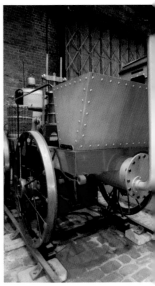

A second Rainhill entrant was *Novelty*, an 0-2-2 well tank built by John Ericsson and John Braithwaite in 1829 and regarded as the first tank engine. This 'version' assembled in 1929 containing many original parts is in the Museum of Science & Industry in Manchester.

In 1980, the Rocket 150 event was staged on the Liverpool & Manchester route, and a working replica of *Novelty* was built by Locomotive Enterprises at the preserved Bowes Railway in County Durham. In 1982, it was sold to the Swedish Railway Museum, Gävle, returning to Britain for the Llangollen 'rematch.'

Timothy Hackworth's *Sans Pareil* was bought by the Liverpool & Manchester Railways after the trials. The remains of the original are housed at Locomotion at Shildon.

The Locomotion museum also has this 1980-built working replica of *Sans Pareil*.

The winner of both the Rainhill Trials and the 'replay' at Llangollen was George Stephenson's *Rocket*. It revolutionised steam haulage by combining the key technologies of blastpipe sand multi-tube boilers and turned colliery locomotives into engines capable of serving the world's first inter-city railway.

Significantly rebuilt after the trials, after retirement from the Liverpool & Manchester Railway, *Rocket* ran on Lord Carlisle's Railway in Cumberland. In 1862 it was donated to the Patent Office Museum in London and is now in the Science Museum.

Today's working replica of *Rocket* was built by engineer Mike Satow and Locomotive Enterprises in 1979 for the Rainhill 150th anniversary celebrations in 1980. It is based at the National Railway Museum in York and is seen visiting the East Lancashire Railway.

The National Railway Museum also has a 'cutaway' replica of *Rocket* and two Liverpool & Manchester Railway carriages in the Great Hall at York.

French engineer Marc Seguin, a major influence on the Stephensons, patented a multi-tubular boiler in 1827 and two years later fitted one to a steam locomotive which became the first to run in France, on the St Etienne-Lyon Railway. This modern-day French replica is seen visiting the Kent & East Sussex Railway.

Invicta, built by Robert Stephenson in Newcastle in 1829 immediately after *Rocket*, was supplied to the Canterbury & Whitstable Railway, hauling the inaugural train on May 3 1830. Retired in 1836 as the railway switched to cable haulage by stationary engines, it became the world's first preserved locomotive. In recent years it has been displayed in Canterbury Museum.

Planet, a 2-2-0 built by Robert Stephenson in 1830 for the Liverpool & Manchester Railway, was the first locomotive to employ inside cylinders. A working replica was built by the Friends of the Museum of Science and Industry in Manchester in 1992.

This stationary steam winding engine, built by Robert Stephenson in 1833, served the Leicester & Swannington Railway, hauling coal trucks up the 1-in-17 Swannington incline and was used until 1947. It is now in the National Railway Museum at York. Cable haulage of passenger trains was first used on the London & Blackwall Railway, engineered by Robert Stephenson and opened in 1840.

Der Adler, a 2-2-2 built by the Stephensons for the Bavarian Ludwigsbahn between Nuremberg and Fürth, made its inaugural run on December 7 1835 and was the first steam locomotive to run commercially in Germany. Scrapped in 1857, a working replica built in 1935 is in the Deutsche Bahn museum in Nuremberg.

Lion is an 0-4-2 built for the Liverpool &
Manchester Railway in 1837 by Todd, Kitson
& Laird. Used in the film *The Titfield
Thunderbolt* in 1952 and is now in the care
of Liverpool's museum service. *Lion* returned
to the Liverpool–Manchester main line for
the Rocket 150 celebrations in 1980 and
is seen passing Golborne on May 18.

This archive view depicts *Lion*
on display at Lime Street station.

Great Western Railway engineer Isambard Kingdom Brunel rejected George Stephenson's 4ft 8½in (standard) gauge in favour of his own bigger 7ft 0¼in gauge, allowing faster locomotives and bigger loadings. The first GWR engine was *North Star*, supplied by Robert Stephenson. On May 31 1838 it worked the inaugural train from Paddington. Preserved at Swindon in 1871, it was controversially scrapped in 1906, but a nonworking replica using surviving parts was assembled in 1923, and is now displayed in STEAM – Museum of the Great Western Railway in Swindon.

The GWR's first locomotive engineer, Daniel Gooch, built his own engines, beginning with the broad gauge express passenger *Firefly* 2-2-2s in 1840. All 62 were withdrawn by 1879, and none survive. A project to build a working replica of *Fire Fly* started by the late Royal Navy Commander John Mosse in 1982, was completed at Didcot Railway Centre in 2005.

Left:
First class travel behind the
new *Fire Fly*, 1840s style.

Right:
A section of Brunel's 7ft 0¼in
broad gauge trackwork recreated
at Didcot Railway Centre.

In April 1847, the first of Gooch's Iron Duke express passenger 4-2-2s, *Iron Duke*, emerged from Swindon Works. None survive, but in 1985 a working replica was built using parts from two standard gauge Hunslet Austerity 0-6-0 saddle tanks for the Great Western 150 celebrations. It is now in the National Railway Museum in York.

Bradyll, built by Timothy Hackworth at his Soho Works in Shildon in 1840 for the South Hetton Railway in County Durham, is the oldest surviving 0-6-0. Currently at Locomotion at Shildon, new research suggests it may not be *Bradyll* but *Nelson*, a locomotive built c1840 by Thomas Richardson of Hartlepool.

Above:
Only the tender of Stockton & Darlington Railway Collier 0-6-0 No 18 *Etherley*, built by William Lister at Darlington in 1840, survives. It is kept at Locomotion.

Right:
Based on Timothy Hackworth's 0-6-0 Royal George, *Derwent* was built in 1845 for the Stockton & Darlington Railway, with tenders at the front and back. Preserved in 1898 it is now in Head of Steam – Darlington Railway Museum a few yards from its Hopetown birthplace.

In 1845, 2-2-2 No 49 *Columbine* became one of the first locomotives to be built at the Crewe Works of the Grand Junction Railway, the world's first trunk railway when it opened in 1837. *Columbine* ran until 1902 and is now in the Science Museum.

London & North Western Railway high-speed express passenger locomotive No 3020 *Cornwall* was designed by Francis Trevithick, son of Richard Trevithick, built at Crewe in 1847 as a 4-2-2 and rebuilt as 2-2-2 in 1858. Still in service in 1925, it is now displayed at Locomotion in Shildon, where it is pictured alongside a 1914 LNWR charabanc.

Left:
Steam trains might have become obsolete as early as the middle of the 19th century had Isambard Kingdom Brunel's bold experiment, with atmospheric traction on the South Devon Railway between Exeter and Newton Abbot between 1847-8 been successful. The system, illustrated here near Dawlish, had engineless trains running at speeds of up to 70mph.

Brunel's atmospheric trains were hauled by a piston connected to a vacuum in a huge pipe between the rails. However, the leather flap which kept the vacuum in the pipe perished in the seaside air, and was also said to have been eaten by rats, bringing Brunel's expensive futuristic experiment to an end. This rare surviving section of pipe is displayed at Didcot Railway Centre in Oxfordshire.

Three Brunel pumping stations in which stationary steam engines pumped out the air from the pipe to create the vacuum survive. This one at Starcross is now used as a yacht club store, while the others are at Torre and Totnes.

Built in 1846 for the Furness Railway, *Coppernob*, an 0-4-0 tender engine named after its distinctive firebox dome, was designed by Edward Bury, Locomotive Superintendent of the London & Birmingham Railway. Retired in 1898 and displayed at Barrow-in-Furness station, World War Two bomb debris left distinctive dents in the dome. It is now in the National Railway Museum in York.

In 1851, London & North Western Railway Southern Division locomotive superintendent J E McConnell designed a series of powerful 2-2-2 express engines called 'Bloomers'.

A non-working replica 'Bloomer' numbered 1009 and named *The Wolvertonian* was commissioned by Milton Keynes Development Corporation for display at the new town's Station Square. It was constructed in 1991 by engineering students and craftsmen in nearby Wolverton Works, the LNWR workshops which built 'Bloomers' first time round. It is seen being returned to Wolverton for overhaul and permanent display.

A fully-working 'Bloomer' replica, No 670, has been taking shape at Tyseley Locomotive Works at Birmingham Railway Museum over the past 20 years as time and funds permit.

Their nickname 'Bloomer' came from Womens' Liberation protagonist Mrs Amelia Bloomer, who shocked Victorian society by seeking to reform contemporary female clothing so that underwear could be glimpsed. These locomotives unashamedly showed all their wheels.

Shannon is the sole surviving standard gauge locomotive built by George England and Co. of New Cross, London. Supplied new to the Sandy & Potton Railway in 1857, it was later bought by the Wantage Tramway in Oxfordshire where it became No 5. The Great Western Railway preserved it at Wantage Road station. It is now stored at Didcot Railway Centre.

This second-class Bodmin & Wadebridge Railway coach comprised two box-like compartments with oil lamps and wooden bench seating. The line's early coaches had leather buffers filled with horsehair.

Left and front cover:

The oldest working standard gauge steam engine in Britain is Furness Railway 0-4-0 No 20. Built in 1863 by Sharp Stewart & Co. of Manchester as one of eight tender locomotives, the rapid growth of freight traffic soon rendered them obsolete, and in 1870 six were sold to the Barrow Haematite Steel Company and were converted by Sharp Stewart into humble saddle tanks without tenders.

Renumbered 7, No 20 continued in traffic until 1960, when it was presented to a special school in Barrow. Bought privately in 1983, it was later rebuilt to its original condition complete with new tender by the Furness Railway Trust. The 'new' engine steamed for the first time in January 1999 and entered service on the Lakeside & Haverthwaite Railway, an old Furness branch.

Its surviving sister, No 25, has been acquired for restoration in its latter-day guise as industrial saddle tank No 6.

In 1863/64, George England supplied four 0-4-0 saddle tanks to the Ffestiniog Railway. They were the first truly successful 1ft 11½ in (narrow) gauge engines built. Three survive, No 1 *Princess*, No 2 *Prince* and No 4 *Palmerston*, the latter two being operational. *Prince* is seen in action at the National Railway Museum in York during the Railfest 2004 event.

The diminutive *Pet* was built in 1865 and spent its 64-year working life on the 18in gauge internal system at Crewe Works. It is now in the National Railway Museum in York.

The only surviving complete original locomotive from Brunel's broad gauge empire is *Tiny*, an 0-4-0 vertical-boilered engine supplied by Sara and Company to the South Devon Railway for dockside working in 1863 and used until 1883. It is now in the museum at Buckfastleigh on the modern-day South Devon Railway.

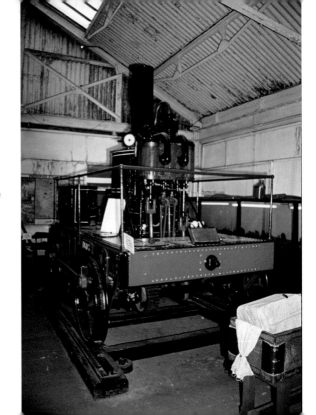

In 1869 George England built the first double-ended *Little Wonder* Fairlie patent articulated 0-4-0+0-4-0T for the tightly-curving Ffestiniog Railway. *Little Wonder* was scrapped in 1882, but the railway continued to use double Fairlies: the oldest still in operation, *Merddyn Emrys*, dates from 1879. Double Fairlie *Livingston Thompson* of 1885 is now on display in the National Railway Museum at York.

Livingston Thompson at Tan-y-Bwlch on the Ffestiniog Railway in 1988.

London & North Western Railway 0-4-0 saddle tank No 1439,
built in 1865, is now on display at Locomotion in Shildon.

In 1979, the Ffestiniog Railway built a brand new double Fairlie, *Earl of Merioneth*, based on the original concept, and another, *David Lloyd George* (pictured), in 1992. A single replica Fairlie 0-4-0T *Taliesin*, based on the scrapped 1876 original, followed in 1999.